How Not to Be an A-Hole Husband and Lose Your Wife
(A Ridiculously Easy 30-Day Guide)

by Brian Ronalds

Forward:

Before writing this book, I was thinking, "How the hell am I going to keep a man's attention on a book about relationships?" In this day and age of smartphones and the Internet, who has time to actually sit down and read a stupid book about how to treat your significant other? Screw statistics, but they do show that the average consumer is accustomed to receiving their news in 140 characters or less and watching videos no more than 10 minutes in length. So, I'm going to do just that — keep it short, simple and ridiculously easy to implement. Believe me, as much as you don't want to read a 500-page book on how to be Prince Charming, I sure as shit don't want to write one!

Before we begin, I would like to dedicate this book to all the A-Hole husbands, boyfriends and any other dipshits that now realize their A-Hole-ness and have changed. Congrats, dudes! It's not easy; in fact you've probably lost some of the most important people in your life due to being a dick. It hurts, bad! I know. I was married for 17 years and lost the girl I thought I'd forever spend my life with.

Crazy epidemic we're facing nowadays. Husbands are sticking around in their marriages, while woman are slamming the doors with middle fingers in the air, never to turn back again. It used to be the man leaving, never to be heard from again. Well, that's not the case anymore. So, what the hell is going on? Let me tell ya … you didn't treat your wife the way she needed to be treated, you moron! More than likely, you used your words for more harm than good. I was once told that women are like glass houses, and cruel words are like stones. The more stones you throw, the more you break that glass house down until there's nothing left. I thought that sounded like a big pile of shit at the time too, but for the most part, it is indeed true.

So listen up! If she hasn't left yet, then it's not too late. Let me help save you from the most excruciating pain your little heart could ever feel. This couldn't be any easier for heaven's sake. Read one measly page a day for the next 30 days and remedy the heartache before you have any! It's really not that difficult. In fact, it's ridiculously easy.

Day 1
Don't Be an A-Hole!

Who me? I'm not an A-Hole! Guess what dudes, if you're reading this, you probably are fellow A-Holes. This is by no means a friggin lecture, but it's definitely time for a change. Start by not being impatient with her. No more taking your bad day out on her. And tell her how amazing dinner was. Most of all, look into her eyes, tell her that you love her, and kiss that sexy mouth of hers! Who knows, you might even get laid! Over the next 30 days, we'll go on a little journey together to figure out why we're so great at being an A-Hole and not so great at being the kind, gentle knight in shining armor that she married. Some days, we will just examine the crucial changes necessary to avoid losing your wife, and other days we'll be putting this plan into action.

So here we go. We'll keep it simple on Day 1, because on this special day we finally realize it's time for change.

Day 2
It's Not All About You

It seems a lot of the time it's all about ME! ME! ME! That's how we are, right? Our work, our badass dreams, our insanely huge and hungry beer guts. But guess what, it's not all about you. Make it about her, too. Ask her how *her* day was. Notice the enticing perfume *she's* wearing. Try and make it a point to cook for *her* at least once a week. She'll love it. A little effort goes hella far. And, be funny! We obviously have a sense of humor; otherwise we wouldn't have even picked up this ridiculously easy guide in the first place.

Day 3
Make Her Numero Uno

So you clearly know now that it's not all about you, right? You better know, otherwise you skipped Day 2 and you're already screwing the pooch! But you wouldn't do that. You're focused on your A-Game, and you remember you're doing this because you don't want to be left by the woman you want to be with forever. She WILL leave, so listen up! She is your number one, your princess, your friend, your lover. I don't care if you've been married for one year or fifty years. Tonight you're going to do the dishes. Although words are nice, what you do is far cooler than what you say.

Day 4
STFU

You know what that means, right — STFU? Probably not, because you're always running your mouth and trying to be 'right.' So take it from me — **S**hut **T**he **F**uck **U**p! Because guess what? There's never a perfect marriage. You will argue and you will say things that you'll regret. So zip it up, put a sock in it. No one has ever been wrong for being silent. Try it! Do her and you a favor, listen to her without having the answer already running in your head. You just might hear what she is actually saying.

Day 5
It's 100%, Not 50%

Have you ever heard someone say, "Meet you halfway there?" That's bullshit in a marriage. You meet her all the way there. I guarantee if you will, she will. So what if you had a hard day at work? She probably did, too. Give her your all! She deserves it, and you deserve it, too. You don't want to be left in the dust from an accumulation of times you could've given your 100% but didn't. Because guess what, she might not ever tell you until it's too late. And dudes, believe me, that's the last thing you want.

Day 6
Listen! Listen! Listen!

Let's see, can I say it one more time without yelling?! Sorry. I can't! *L I S T E N TO HER!!!* We spend our lives talking more than listening, it's no wonder when she tells you something life changing and important that you hear the words, but don't truly listen. Remember when you first started dating her? You'd hold on to every word, every syllable, every exclamation. This communication, called listening, is a tool to let her know that you're engaged, that you care. It's such a simple thing. So when she talks to you, put down whatever the hell you're doing, look straight into her eyes, and fucking listen!

Day 7
Foreplay

I know, I know, you might have to google this one because you probably don't know what it means, and if you do, you more than likely suck at it. Even if you think you're king at this, you're not. Sorry. You can't just hop on top of her naked body and pray that she'll be dripping wet by the time you shove yourself inside her. Use your hands, your mouth. And not just for five minutes. Go down, and go to town. When's the last time you went down for 20-30 minutes? Ever? This is a must. Kiss her neck and use your hands until she can't stand it anymore. Let her initiate your manliness by grabbing it and putting it inside her. When she does this, you'll have immediate affirmation and know you rocked it!

Day 8
S E X

How often do you have sex? I agree, everyone isn't the same, but banging your wife is a huge part of your marriage. When I say "banging," I mean "making love." So bang away, gentlemen! Most men in marriages don't take their wives on the baloney train anywhere near as often as their wives would prefer. This is a big deal. She wants to feel wanted! She wants to feel sexy. Simply … she wants to get banged! Remember though, before you engage in the horizontal hula, buzzing the brillo, burying the bone, the ol' lust and thrust, threading that needle, stuffing the turkey and rocking the Kasbah, refer to day 7.

Day 9
Respect

In everything you do, in everything you say, respect this human that gives her life to you every day. But how, you ask? Open the car door for her. That'll really freak her out. Peel the carrots at suppertime for her. She might pass out. Do the laundry for her. Rub her feet. Write her a poem. Even when she's not there, talk about her at work like she's the princess you've always dreamed of. Get off the computer with your cock in your hand, and go get on your wife. That's right homies. Ease up a tad on the porn! To some, it's considered disrespectful and unrealistic. It may cause damage to your heart, mind, body and soul. Your wife is your porn star; she wants to be, so let her.

Day 10
Appreciate All That She Does

Did you notice that she just got a haircut and changed her color? How about the new perfume she's wearing? Are those new sexy high heels that make her legs look like they go on for miles? Guess what? It's for you. Did you notice? Did you tell her that you noticed? This is huge, fellas! Appreciate all the things she does great and small. How about that dinner she cooked? Was she trying something new? It actually might have sucked and tasted awful, but do you tell her? Hell no! You appreciate the effort. Pay attention to everything, because the moment you stop will be the moment she stops and the moment someone else will notice for you. And this, my A-hole friends, could be the beginning of the end. Appreciate everything all the way down to the new pink lacey G-string she just bought ... for you, we hope.

Day 11
Love

Wuv, Twue Wuv! Isn't that all we need? Mostly, but did you know that everyone has a different love language? There are 5: Words of Affirmation, Acts of Service, Receiving Gifts, Quality Time and Physical Touch. Do you know yours? More importantly, do you know hers? She may have all five in some sense. So get off your ass and tell her you love her, wash her car and fill up the gas tank. Spoil her panties off with some gifts, take her for a walk and after all that, give her a body massage ending with fucking her brains out. I mean, making love.

Day 12
Adore Her

Invest in her happiness. Tell her how much you adore her every day. She wants to know that you love and appreciate her. And don't just tell her how much; tell her *why* you adore her. Know what her dreams are. Encourage them. The more you support them, the more she'll want you to be a part of them. Make her your top priority. No one wants to play second best. Accept this woman and cherish her for the person she is. Honestly fellas, if you can't do these things for her, she'll find someone who will. So don't fuck it up. You get one shot in this life to be the man you need to be in your marriage!

Day 13
Give Her Your Quality Time

Quality time with your girl is such a BFD (Big Fucking Deal)! It seems so damn simple, but this very little thing can be overlooked and forgotten about through time. Special time together presents many opportunities for growth in a relationship, and shouldn't be optional. This shit is required, dudes! It's these unique times where we form a deeper connection. Here are a few simple suggestions:

Cook together. Have you ever done that? It's badass and quite romantic. Play cards. Hold hands regularly. Snuggle together and watch a movie. Guess what happens during snuggle time?!! Mm Hmmm. That's right — SEX! The ultimate quality time! Just don't forget Day 7. When in doubt, refer to Day 7!

Day 14
Help Her Around the House

This is so easy but so oftentimes forgotten. I mean, how hard is it to vacuum or take the dishes out of the dishwasher? It not only helps clean your home, but it shows your wife that you love her. I know you can't do this every day, but how about a couple times a week? How cool would you be if you walked in from a long hard day at work, make out with your hot wife, pour her a glass of wine, sit her down, and let her watch you vacuum, dust, and tidy up the house? You'll have her bragging to all of her friends, and guess what? You're learning how to be the perfect husband, the man she can't stop thinking about.

Day 15
Affection Is What She Wants

Holy shit! You're on Day 15! Halfway through your 30-day guide and closer to becoming the man that you are, but just didn't know how to be. Now, this is an important day, so listen up! Here are 5 simple ways to be affectionate instantly. In fact, after you read this day, apply what you've learned as soon as possible. 1.) Write her a small note (max 3 sentences) and put it in a place she'll later see. 2.) Hugs, you can't ever give out too many hugs, it's friggin impossible! 3.) Compliment her; how she looks, how the house looks, what a great Mom she is. Whatever, it's simple. 4.) Bring her flowers. I know, totally cliché, but it wouldn't be a cliché if it wasn't true. She'll dig it. 5.) Tell her you love her. She can't hear it enough.

Day 16
Use Kind Words

This is huge, guys. No matter what, never ever, ever, ever call her names!! When you call her names, you might as well throw your marriage right down the shitter. Remember, women are like glass houses, and name calling and hurtful words are like rocks. The more rocks you throw, the more you shatter her inner being into not wanting to be with you. Try some of these kind words on for size; they'll make her heart happy.

"You make me want to be a better man," "You're fun to be with," "You're meal was amazing," "My most favorite place to be is with you," "I love your smile," and how about, "You make me a happy man!" If you're not use to saying these things, it might be a challenge at first, but you're going to get good at this, damn good!

Day 17
Kindness

Small acts of kindness are investments into your future love bank with your wife. We touched base yesterday on using your words for kindness, now let's build your expertise on showing her. Here's the deal, without showing kindness to your wife, your marriage will not last. How about saying "Yes" more than saying "No"? That's a huge start. When you listen to her, use your ears of course, but even more so, listen with your heart. Make it a habit to look for the good in her instead of the bad. When she's speaking, don't interrupt her. Be polite! Remember you're well on your way from ridding yourself from the land of A-Holes, so apply these random acts of kindness. She'll adore you for it!

Day 18
Fight Fair

So, of course, you've figured out that there is no such thing as a perfect marriage. Show me a perfect marriage and I'll show you a couple that's not only full of secrets, but full of shit, too! You're going to fight, so fight fair. I know it's difficult, but try to always stay calm. You won't remedy anything with a flared temper. I know, it seems impossible and in the heat of the moment it's tough. But you're an adult, and not only that, you love and adore the person that's getting on your nerves at that time. So chill the fuck out. Be clear of what the issue is and try not to fight through the late hours of the night. You'll wake up feeling like shit and not even remembering what the hell you were fighting about! Most importantly, make an effort by not hitting below the belt. You know your wife and all her vulnerabilities better than anyone else so don't use those things against her. It's uncool and not fair.

Day 19
Get to REALLY Know Her

So hopefully you know her birthday, her favorite place to shop and her favorite drink. If not, boy oh boy, you've got some serious work to do. And you're kind of a dumbass. But don't take that the wrong way, it's all out of love! Seriously though, do you know her favorite color, her favorite food, her favorite thing to do? What is she most grateful for in life? If she could go anywhere in the world, where would it be? What's her favorite restaurant, her favorite funny movie? Is she really happy in her personal growth, or does she want to go back to school? Does she desire a promotion at work? You wouldn't believe the things you don't know about the person you eat with and sleep next to every single day. This is an easy day for you. You know why? Because all you have to do is fucking ask! This will bring her so much closer to you and show her that you care about what she loves and desires.

Day 20
Stability

This day is a bit of a toughie because levels of stability for women differentiate from one to the other. For some women, emotional stability is far more important than financial stability, and vice versa. So it's your job to find out which one is more important to her. To be safe, find a good balance of both. I know jobs come and go, and it can be tough on us guys sometimes, but to make it easier on her and you, create an "Oh Shit Fund" just in case things go awry. That will bring her peace. As far as emotional stability is concerned, as long as you're following and implementing Days 1-20 at this point, you're golden.

Day 21
Make Her Laugh

Wow! 10 days left, guys, and you've been following this guide so well, she's practically throwing her panties at you when you walk through the door. Well done. She may hardly even recognize you anymore because she's more in love with you today than the day you got married. And that's exactly what you want. Now, if she's not tossing those panties around just yet, you can actually get her naked by being the hilarious husband that you can be. Let's face it, even if you're an ugly dude, if you can make a girl laugh you can steal her heart away. So be funny and silly, and lighten your ass up.

Day 22
Be a Man

Don't take that the wrong way, guys! I know you're a man, but does she? Yes, you have a penis, you can lift heavy things, and your deep manly voice is sexy and authoritative. But do you know how to be *her* man? Let me encourage you to give her the feeling that you would do anything to make her feel safe. She wants that. She needs it. She wants you to be nice but also her knight in shining armor. When she's upset or sad, comfort her and let her know that everything will be all right. When you're together, how about putting your arm around her waist and not her shoulder? Be a confident man. Don't be a pussy! Women love confidence. Don't overdo it with the confidence, though, by acting arrogant or egotistical, that'll go against everything you're working towards.

Day 23
Make Her Feel Pretty and Sexy

It may be possible that I'm sounding like a broken record. But repetition is healthy. When you create a memory or perform an act, a pathway is created between your brain cells. It's kind of like taking a stroll through a hella crazy forest. When you first attempt to make your way through the rubbish, you have to fight your ass through the undergrowth. But once you feel comfort through the road untraveled, it becomes second nature, and that's what we're trying to get through to our thick skulls. Make her feel sexy! Smell and kiss her neck, tell her she smells good (and it's not the perfume) and relish in the moment. Such a small act will entice her. Tell her that her smile is so damn pretty that you can't help to kiss that mouth of hers. When you hug her, hold on like you never want to let go. Don't forget that you picked her and only her to spend the rest of your life with.

Day 24
Be Present

Living in the moment and being forever present could be one of the most important things you can do in your life for her. It's impossible to watch TV, work on your computer or text someone while having a conversation. Not only is it impossible, it's fucking rude. I get it, our lives are super busy. So do one or the other, not both. Could you imagine if you were having sex with your wife and while you were all up inside her she whips out her tablet and replies to an email? You'd not only have a conniption, you might have a heart attack at the same time. When you're with her, make her the only one that matters. It's like the old phrase, "Stop and smell the roses." Your wife is your rose, so stop what you're doing, and for the love of God, smell her.

Day 25
The Nagging – The Damn Nagging

Stop the nagging. Yours, not hers. This all goes back to being kind with your words. If you've gotten this far, you're truly dedicated into getting out from swimming in the A-Hole pool and jumping into the fountain of kindness, consideration and love. Well done.

But the nagging has got to stop. Why isn't dinner ready? This house is a complete disaster! Why haven't you done the laundry? That's not the way to fold my shirts! Why didn't you fill up the gas tank? You know what I'm talking about men. This shit has got to stop. Use your words to build her up, and instead of looking for things she may not have done, focus on the things she has accomplished in her day, and tell her! It sucks, but humans tend to remember the shitty things that happen in their lives more so than the good things. So fill her cup of life with so many good memories, that it will be all she remembers when she thinks about you.

Day 26
Understand Her Needs

If you haven't figured this one out yet, it's time. It goes back to understanding her love languages. Remember them? There are 5. I'll tell you again: Words of Affirmation, Acts of Service, Receiving Gifts, Quality Time and Physical Touch. Not only are these important to know about your wife, but it's also important to understand other needs she desires from you and from life. She wants to know what your vital needs are. Have you told her? Women tend to find purpose and security in knowing that she is meeting *your needs* in a way that no other woman could. Most of all, she wants to be cherished and adored. Sit her down over a glass of wine, and learn her love languages. This, too, my friends will get you laid. Guaranteed.

Day 27
Honesty

Honesty in a marriage is non-negotiable. Period. Whether it's money, the people you're sharing your time with, the things that you do when she is not around, it all matters and she needs to know. So what if you tell a teeny tiny white lie like skipping out on your diet for the day? It may feel shitty at first, but over time, the second, third, fourth white lie gets easier and easier, and you suddenly become desensitized from the truth; numb. Lies destroy trust in a marriage. You want her to tell you the truth, right? Wouldn't you want to know that she was hanging out at the park once a week with her old male pal from high school? Hell yeah, you would! In fact, you probably wouldn't like it one fucking bit. The exact same thing applies to you. Of course you can still be the independent man that you are, but it all comes down to character, which is often defined by what you do when people aren't looking. "The true test of a man's character is what he does when no one is watching." –John Wooden

Day 28
Don't Compartmentalize

A wise man I know once said that our lives should be less like TV dinners and more like pot pies. The way we behave and handle ourselves at work, school and home should be the same across the board. Webster's defines the term compartmentalize as 'the ability to separate into isolated compartments or categories.' It is unhealthy to separate and isolate different parts of our worlds from our wives.

Withholding information about our lives from your spouse is untruthful, and is in fact a lie. This is a great way to really fuck up your marriage. So simply be honest with yourself and avoid this self-destruction before it's too late.

Day 29
Pay Attention

Make every moment count — from when you wake up to when you snuggle next to her before bedtime. Don't forget, guys, this is the woman you vowed to spend the rest of your life with. Make some effort! Pay attention when she talks and to what she says, how she smiles, how she hugs and kisses you, how she raises your children, how she laughs, how she sings, how she acts silly, how she gives you love. Notice all these amazing things that made her that special human who stole your heart away. You're a lucky ass man to have found her, don't let the day-to-day go by without noticing what makes her, her.

Day 30
The First Date

Holy shit! We did it! It's day friggin 30. Congrats! On your final day, I want you to go back, way back to your very first date. What you did, what you said, how you acted and how you felt. I'm pretty sure you were trying to impress her skirt off, and in most cases, you probably did. So, take her back to the first day again. Retrace that date. Look at her for the first time with fresh eyes. This time however, you're equipped with some of the best tools you could have in being a great husband. You can feel great in knowing that the girl of your dreams is happy and is going to stay happy! Rest assured, on *this* "first date," you know you're getting laid at the end of the night. And why the hell not … you deserve it!

Afterword:

Here's the deal: Marriage takes work. If you're not willing to work at it, I promise that you will live a miserable life. You've probably noticed by now, if you're making just a little effort and implementing the 30-day plan, you'll see drastic changes within yourself, and in her. Has she begun to compliment and give you back her flirty eyes again? Treat her as you want to be treated and YOU, my friend, will be treated to more blowies! Once you step up you're A-Game again, she'll come up to bat.

By now, you know you don't want to be an A-Hole husband; and by now, you know how not to be one. So come on back from time-to-time to this ridiculously easy 30-day guide, and brush up your skills. Rid yourself from being an A-Hole husband, and more importantly, rid yourself of the possibilities of losing your wife.

Made in the USA
Columbia, SC
09 November 2021

48627955R00036